I0448537

JUNE 03

Batterer Intervention Programs

Where Do We Go From Here?

Shelly Jackson, Lynette Feder,
David R. Forde, Robert C. Davis,
Christopher D. Maxwell, and
Bruce G. Taylor

NCJ 195079

Sarah V. Hart

Director

Findings and conclusions of the research reported here are those of the authors and do not reflect the official position or policies of the U.S. Department of Justice.

The studies discussed in this report were supported by the National Institute of Justice under grants 94–IJ–CX–0047 and 96–WT–NX–0008.

The National Institute of Justice is a component of the Office of Justice Programs, which also includes the Bureau of Justice Assistance, the Bureau of Justice Statistics, the Office of Juvenile Justice and Delinquency Prevention, and the Office for Victims of Crime.

About This Report

Batterer intervention programs were introduced as a way to hold batterers accountable without incarcerating them. Initial studies suggested that the programs reduced battering. Two evaluations of programs in Broward County, Florida, and Brooklyn, New York, based on more rigorous experimental designs, claim that they have little or no effect.

There are two possible explanations for these findings. One is that the evaluations may be methodologically flawed; the other is that something may be wrong with the programs themselves. This report analyzes both possibilities and suggests directions for future policy and research.

What did the researchers find?

In the Broward County study, no significant differences were found between batterers in the treatment and control groups on reoffense rates or attitudes toward domestic violence. In the Brooklyn study, the results were more complicated: Men who completed an 8-week treatment program showed no differences from the control group, but men who had completed a 26-week program had significantly fewer official complaints lodged against them than the control group. No difference was found among the three groups in attitudes toward domestic violence.

What were the studies' limitations?

In both studies, response rates were low, many people dropped out of the program, and victims could not be found for subsequent interviews. The tests used to measure batterers' attitudes toward domestic violence and their likelihood to engage in future abuse were of questionable validity. In the Brooklyn study, random assignment was overridden to a significant extent, which makes it difficult to attribute effects exclusively to the program.

Who should read this report?

Administrators of batterer intervention programs, advocates, and researchers.

Contents

Batterer Intervention Programs

Shelly Jackson

With the establishment of proarrest policies in the 1980s, increasing numbers of batterers were seen in criminal courts across the country. Initially, they were sentenced to jail. Some victims, however, began to say that although they wanted the battering to stop, they did not want their partners incarcerated. To respond to these requests while still holding batterers accountable, offenders were referred to batterer intervention programs (BIPs, also known as spouse abuse abatement programs or SAAPs).[1] This has led researchers and advocates to ask, "Do these programs work?"

Although early evaluations suggested that BIPs reduce battering, recent evaluations based on more rigorous designs find little or no reduction. The methodological limitations of virtually all these evaluations, however, make it impossible to say how effective BIPs are.

About the Author

Shelly Jackson is a program manager in NIJ's Office of Research and Evaluation.

This NIJ Special Report describes the results of two recent evaluations that add to this growing literature. Lynette Feder and David Forde in Broward County, Florida, and Robert Davis, Bruce Taylor, and Christopher Maxwell in Brooklyn, New York, conducted experimental evaluations of programs based on the Duluth model (see "Types of batterer intervention programs"). The Brooklyn evaluation found some reductions in battering, but it found no evidence that the program had any effect on batterers' attitudes. The Broward County evaluation found no change in either behavior or attitudes. These evaluations are described in detail below.

Types of batterer intervention programs

The first BIP models were psychoeducational programs. One such program, the Duluth model, is based on the feminist theory that patriarchal ideology, which encourages men to control their partners, causes domestic violence. The Duluth model helps men confront their attitudes about control and teaches them other strategies for dealing with their partners. This model is the most common form of BIP in the Nation; many States mandate that BIPs conform to the Duluth model.

There are several alternatives to the Duluth model.[2] Cognitive-behavioral intervention views battering as a result of errors in thinking and focuses on skills training and anger management.[3] Another model, group practice, works from the premise that battering has multiple causes and therefore combines a psychoeducational curriculum, cognitive-behavioral techniques, and an assessment of individual needs.[4] Examples of these programs include Emerge and AMEND (Abusive Men Exploring New Directions).[5]

Programs based on batterer typologies or profiles—most commonly psychological and criminal-justice–based typologies[6]—are gaining popularity.[7] BIPs based on these profiles are just beginning to be developed and have not been evaluated.[8]

Another, more controversial, intervention is couples therapy. This model views

men and women as equal participants in creating disturbances in the relationship. Although couples therapy may be appropriate for some people, it is widely criticized for inappropriately assigning the woman a share of the blame for the continuation of violence.[9]

Review of batterer intervention program evaluations

More than 35 BIP evaluations have been published. Early studies, which used quasi-experimental designs, consistently found small program effects; when more methodologically rigorous evaluations were undertaken, the results were inconsistent and disappointing.[10] Most of the later studies found that treatment effects were limited to a small reduction in reoffending,[11] although evidence indicates that for most participants (perhaps those already motivated to change), BIPs may end the most violent and threatening behaviors.[12] The results, however, remain inconclusive because of methodological flaws in these evaluations.[13]

Although most of the programs evaluated followed the Duluth model, cognitive-behavior therapy has also been examined. In 21 of 24 controlled studies, reoffense rates were lower among program participants than among the control group (although not all differences were statistically significant).[14] These effects were larger in demonstration programs (implemented by a researcher) than in practical programs (implemented by a juvenile or criminal justice agency) or a combination of the two. This suggests that the way a program is put into practice (i.e., how faithful it is to the intervention model) may be key in determining its impact. Outcomes were measured only for an

average of 20 weeks after the end of treatment, which did not allow an assessment of longer term reoffense rates.

Differences in evaluation methods account for much of the inconsistency in findings. Pure experimental designs, favored by researchers because of their methodological rigor, make finding true effects easier and reduce the likelihood of error but are challenging to carry out in the field; as a result, design flaws may cast doubt on the results. Quasi-experimental designs, which differ from pure experiments in that group assignment is not random, are easier to carry out but are more open to misinterpretation. Thus, it is hard to tell whether program effects are true or masked because the evaluation was compromised in the field.

The next two chapters present the results of recent BIP evaluations in Broward County, Florida, and Brooklyn, New York. Both studies used classical experimental designs: Batterers were randomly assigned to experimental or control groups. In Broward County, men in the experimental group were sentenced to 1 year of probation and 26 weeks of group counseling at a BIP, whereas men in the control group were sentenced to 1 year of probation. In Brooklyn, due to circumstances discussed in detail in the chapter devoted to that study, some men in the experimental group received their treatment in 26 weekly sessions, while others attended longer, twice-weekly sessions for 8 weeks. Men assigned to the control group took part in a community service program. In both studies, the two groups were tested to see whether treatment had changed their attitudes toward violence. Recidivism was measured both by official measures and by victim reports of abuse. In Broward County, offender self-reports of abuse were also recorded.

The Broward County study found no significant difference between the experimental and control groups in attitudes toward the role of women, whether wife beating should be a crime, or whether the State had the right to intervene in cases of domestic violence. It also found no significant difference between groups in victims' perceptions of the likelihood that their partners would beat them again. Official measures followed the same pattern: No significant difference was found between groups in violations of probation or rearrests. In fact, men assigned to the experimental group were more likely to be rearrested than members of the control group unless they had attended all of the treatment sessions.

In the Brooklyn study, initial findings showed that the experimental group as a whole was less likely than the control group to be arrested again for a crime against the same victim. On a closer look, however, only the 26-week group had significantly fewer official complaints than the control group at 6 and 12 months. The pattern of victim reports was the same (although the differences between the 8- and 26-week groups were not statistically significant). The study found no difference among the three groups in attitudes toward domestic violence.

These studies, however, suffer from several limitations. Response rates were low and sample attrition high in both studies. The measures of batterers' attitudes toward domestic violence and likelihood to engage in further abuse are of questionable validity. Random assignment to the control group was overridden to a significant extent, especially in the Brooklyn study. Without process evaluations, there is no way to tell how well the Duluth model was being implemented in the treatment sites. These and other limitations and the policy implications of the Broward County and Brooklyn studies are discussed in detail in the final chapter.

Notes

1. Although this report discusses male batterers, women batter as well. It is highly probable, however, that the dynamics of battering differ for males and females, which suggests the need for batterer intervention programs designed specifically to meet the needs of female batterers. Currently, it appears that most women batterers are being placed in male-dominated batterer intervention programs.

2. Healey, K., C. Smith, and C. O'Sullivan, *Batterer Intervention: Program Approaches and Criminal Justice Strategies*, Issues and Practices, Washington, DC: U.S. Department of Justice, National Institute of Justice, February 1998. NCJ 168638.

3. Babcock, J.C., and J.J. La Taillade, "Evaluating Interventions for Men Who Batter," in *Domestic Violence: Guidelines for Research-Informed Practice*, ed. J.P. Vincent and E.N. Jouriles. Philadelphia: Jessica Kingsley Publishers, 2000; Lipsey, M., G. Chapman, and N. Landenberger, "Cognitive-Behavioral Programs for Offenders: A Synthesis of the Research on their Effectiveness for Reducing Recidivism," paper presented at the "Systematic Reviews of Criminological Interventions" conference, Washington, DC, April 2–3, 2001.

4. Babcock, J.C., and J.J. La Taillade, "Evaluating Interventions for Men Who Batter."

5. Healey, K., C. Smith, and C. O'Sullivan, *Batterer Intervention: Program Approaches and Criminal Justice Strategies*.

6. Holtzworth-Munroe, A., and G.L. Stuart, "Typologies of Male Batterers: Three Subtypes and the Differences Among Them," *Psychological Bulletin* 116(3)(1994): 476–97.

7. Healey, K., C. Smith, and C. O'Sullivan, Batterer *Intervention: Program Approaches and Criminal Justice Strategies*.

8. Wexler, D.B., "The Broken Mirror: A Self Psychological Treatment Perspective for Relationship Violence," *Journal of Psychotherapy, Practice, and Research* 8(2)(1999): 129–41.

9. Babcock, J.C. and J.J. La Taillade, "Evaluating Interventions for Men Who Batter."

10. See Babcock, J.C., C.E. Green, and C. Robie, "Does Batterer's Treatment Work? A Meta-Analytic Review of Domestic Violence," *Journal of Family Psychology* (under review); Davis, R.C., and B.G. Taylor, "Does Batterer Treatment Reduce Violence? A Synthesis of the Literature," *Women and Criminal*

Justice 10(2)(1999): 69–93; Tolman, R.M., and J.L. Edleson, "Intervention for Men who Batter: A Review of Research," in *Understanding Partner Violence: Prevalence, Causes, Consequences, and Solutions,* ed. S.R. Stith and M.A. Straus. Minneapolis, MN: National Council on Family Relations, 1995: 262–73.

11. Babcock, J.C., and J.J. La Taillade, "Evaluating Interventions for Men Who Batter."

12. Edleson, J.L., "Controversy and Change in Batterer's Programs," in *Future Interventions with Battered Women and their Families,* ed. J.L. Edleson and Z.C. Eisikovitz. Thousand Oaks, CA: Sage Publications, 1996: 154–169; Gondolf, E.W., "Batterer Programs: What We Know and Need to Know," *Journal of Interpersonal Violence* 12(1)(1997): 83–98.

13. Healey, K., C. Smith, and C. O'Sullivan, *Batterer Intervention: Program Approaches and Criminal Justice Strategies.*

14. Lipsey, M., G. Chapman, and N. Landenberger, "Cognitive-Behavioral Programs for Offenders: A Synthesis of the Research on their Effectiveness for Reducing Recidivism."

The Broward Experiment

Lynette Feder and David R. Forde

Methodology

Selection procedure

This study took place in Broward County, Florida (encompassing Fort Lauderdale), in the two courts charged exclusively with handling domestic violence cases in that jurisdiction. It used a classical experimental design. All men convicted of misdemeanor domestic violence in the county during a 5-month period in 1997 were randomly assigned to experimental or control groups.[1] The only exceptions were:

- Couples in which either defendant or victim did not speak English or Spanish.

- Couples in which either defendant or victim was under 18 years of age or the defendant was severely mentally ill.

- Cases in which the judge allowed the defendant to move to another jurisdiction at the time of sentencing and serve his probation through mail contact.

All other defendants (a total of 404) were assigned randomly to one of the two groups.

Random assignment

Cases were randomly assigned based on the computer-generated court docket number. The judge announced the assignment at the time the defendant was adjudicated. Defendants were placed in the experimental group if their docket number was even and in the control group if it was odd. This method allowed the judges to carry out the process quickly, and it let researchers know when assignments were not random.

Men placed in the experimental group were sentenced to 1 year of probation and 26 weeks of group counseling sessions from a local BIP. Men placed in the control group were sentenced to 1 year of probation only. At sentencing, the judge referred defendants to one of five county-certified batterer treatment programs, each of which used the Duluth model. The county's probation office monitored compliance.

Outcome measures

To capture the true amount of change in individuals undergoing court-mandated counseling, researchers included measures from several sources. Batterers were interviewed at adjudication and again 6 months later. Victims were interviewed at adjudication and 6 and 12 months later. Valid, reliable standardized measures were used whenever possible. Probation records and computer checks with the local police for all new arrests were used to track defendants for 1 year after adjudication.

Hypothesis

Although the study's ultimate purpose was to test whether court-mandated counseling reduced the likelihood of future violence by convicted batterers, it also was designed to test the theory that stake-in-conformity variables (e.g., age, a steady job, marriage to one's partner, a stable residence) could explain when an intervention (an arrest or court-mandated treatment)

About the Authors

Lynette Feder and David R. Forde are associate professors of criminology and criminal justice at the University of Memphis.

would reduce the likelihood of subsequent violence. This study began with two hypotheses:

- Batterers who were mandated to undergo counseling would be less likely to beat their partners again than those assigned to the control group.

- Men with a high stake in conformity would be less likely to beat their partners again than those with a low stake in conformity.

Batterer profile

Age and marital status. Batterers participating in this study ranged from 19 to 71 years of age; the typical offender was 35 years old. Fifty-seven percent were white, 36 percent were black, and 6 percent were Hispanic. Forty-five percent of the batterers said they were married, 43 percent said they were single, and 13 percent said they were separated or divorced.

Education and economic status. Most of the men were long-term Broward County residents who had lived there for an average of 160 months. Twenty-five percent reported that they failed to complete high school; 9 percent said they had graduated from college. Most of the men rented (67 percent) rather than owned (33 percent) their homes. Seventy-two percent reported being employed at the time of adjudication, with most of these saying that they had been at their current job for 2 years or less. Forty-seven percent of the men reported working in an unskilled or semiskilled position; 8 percent reported working as officials and managers. Salaries ranged from $250 to $10,000 per month.

Criminal record. Many of the men had a prior criminal record. Forty percent had one or more misdemeanor arrests (averaging about 0.9 misdemeanor offenses per individual), and 20 percent had one or more felony arrests (averaging 0.3 prior felony arrests per offender). Many had been convicted and jailed (44 percent had one or more jail stays) or imprisoned (7 percent had been imprisoned at least once). For 85 percent of the men in the sample, this was their first arrest for domestic violence.

Police reports noted that approximately 28 percent of the incidents of domestic violence for which the defendants had been convicted or adjudicated involved alcohol; another 3 percent involved drugs. Victim injuries were recorded in 74 percent of the cases. These injuries most often were bruises (58 percent), although 8 percent were severe enough to require the victim's hospitalization. Men were taken into custody 99 percent of the time.

Victim profile

Age and marital status. A profile of the women involved in this study is drawn from responses to the victim survey at the time of adjudication. Victims ranged from 18 to 63 years of age; the typical victim was 34 years old. Women were, on average, 2 years younger than their partners; age differences ranged from 23 years younger to 14 years older. About 53 percent of the women reported that their husbands had battered them; 37 percent said that their live-in boyfriends had battered them. Victims reported that they had been with the batterer an average of 7 years.

Education and economic status. About 23 percent of victims said they had less than a 12th-grade education; about 10 percent were college graduates. Forty-seven percent said they were employed full-time, 19 percent reported part-time employment, 11 percent said they were homemakers, and approximately 3 percent said they were unemployed and looking for a job. Of those who were working, 63 percent reported they were in unskilled or semiskilled positions, and almost 20

percent reported working in professional or managerial positions. Women with better jobs may have been overrepresented in the victim survey sample; 90 percent of these women reported that their husband or boyfriend was working, whereas only 72 percent of the men in the sample reported that they were employed at the time of adjudication.

Treatment delivery measures

Batterers in the experimental group usually were assigned to attend 26 group counseling sessions over 26 weeks. A batterer who missed a session was required to make it up. Almost 29 percent attended all the sessions, and approximately 95 percent missed five or fewer sessions. Eventually, approximately 66 percent attended all of the sessions; about 13 percent attended no classes at all. Of the control group, 97 percent attended no classes.

Outcome measures

Offender and victim interviews used several standardized scales to assess the outcomes of the experiment. These included an abbreviated version of the Inventory of Beliefs About Wife Beating and Attitudes Towards Women. Batterers were also asked whether they believed that their battering should be considered criminal, whether they thought they were responsible, and how likely they were to batter again. The revised Conflict Tactics Scale (CTS2) was used to assess their self-reports of verbal, physical, or sexual abuse within the previous 6 months. Since men assigned to a BIP may not have attended any or all of the sessions, or some not assigned may have attended on their own, data were analyzed in terms of both treatment assigned and treatment received.

Victims were asked about the batterer's behavior, their beliefs about who was

responsible, and whether they thought another battering was likely. Offenders were asked about self-reported partner abuse at time of adjudication and 6 months later. Victims were surveyed at time of adjudication, 6 months later, and 1 year later. At each point, survey data were analyzed for differences between the experimental and control groups to see whether changes occurred over time.

Experimental integrity

Given the problems inherent in running an experiment, the integrity of the experiment as carried out must be addressed.

Outcome of random assignment.
Statistical tests showed that the original random assignments did not differ from chance.[2] Forty-two of the 446 cases (9 percent) were dropped for failing to meet the criteria for inclusion, however, and in another 14 cases (3.5 percent), judges placed men originally assigned into the control group into treatment. This left a total of 188 men (43 percent) in the control group and 216 men (57 percent) in the treatment group. The likelihood of such a large split between the groups is very low.[3]

Equivalence tests at the time of adjudication found no significant differences between the two groups in stake-in-conformity variables (criminal record, the domestic violence incident for which they had been convicted or adjudicated, or offender demographics), with one exception: The control group was 2 years younger than the experimental group. Studies consistently have found that older men are less likely to abuse their partners and to continue battering.[4] Therefore, the observation that men in the control group were significantly younger than those in the experimental group would make it easier to find how effective treatment was.

Survey response rates. Individuals did not volunteer to be part of the experiment, but they could not be interviewed without their consent. Although all defendants who met the criteria were included in the sample, not all defendants and their victims agreed to be interviewed. Many victims who did not respond could not be located; on the other hand, many defendants simply refused to be interviewed.

The low response rate reflects the charged environment in which the experiment was conducted. Vocal opposition to the project led many who had supported the research financially to take a step back. Although they did not actively oppose the research, their failure to deliver their promised support (on which the researchers relied) strained project resources and lowered response rates. Response rates among defendants were 80 percent for the first interview and 50 percent for the second, 6 months after adjudication. Response rates for men in the experimental and control groups were equivalent. Completion rates among victims were even lower: 49 percent for the first interview, 30 percent for the second, and 22 percent for the last. Victims of batterers in the experimental and control groups had no significant difference in response rates. Although low response rates are typical when working with victims of domestic violence,[5] they present a limitation to this study.

As one would expect, it was easier to track defendants' progress through official measures. The research team collected and coded all probation folders (and the information in them) at time of adjudication and coded all but one again 12 months later. As a further check, each defendant's name was run against the computerized files from the county sheriff's office, which contained the records for all arrests in Broward County.

Integrity of experimental and control conditions. The literature gives examples of "compensation," providing the control group with something extra to make up for not receiving the intervention.[6] This threatens internal validity because the control group is no longer a genuine control group (i.e., the two groups are no longer comparable in all ways except that the experimental group receives the intervention).

In this study, researchers tested for this possibility. Since judges had the opportunity to order additional monitoring or supervision for the control group, judicial orders for men in both groups were compared. Judges were found to have assigned equivalent evaluations, supervision, and non-BIP treatment programs to the men in both groups. Since the county probation office could have more closely supervised the men in the control group, the two groups were compared for the following:

- The number of months that they failed to report to the probation office without being cited for violating probation conditions.

- The number of probation meetings scheduled, missed, and rescheduled.

- The number of months for which there were written monthly reports for each probationer.

- Whether they underwent alcohol or drug testing.

- The number of times they were tested.

None of these comparisons were significant or even showed a tendency toward significance; thus, there is no reason to conclude that probation officers treated the two groups differently.

The probation office also might not have sufficiently monitored the attendance of the experimental group. If batterers were

not sufficiently sanctioned for failing to attend treatment, this experiment would not offer a true test of the efficacy of court-mandated counseling. This possibility was investigated by looking at treatment attendance history. Of the 79 men who missed BIP sessions without making them up, 70 (89 percent) were cited for violating probation conditions on one or more occasions. Of the nine (11 percent) who missed BIP sessions and were not cited for violating probation conditions, four had missed only one session and one had missed only two. These results indicate that the probation office adequately monitored attendance and sanctioned batterers for not attending treatment.

Random assignment ensured that the experimental and control groups were comparable before treatment. There is no reason to believe that the two groups did not receive the same amount and kind of monitoring, supervision, and treatment throughout the test period, with the single exception that the experimental group was mandated to attend BIP counseling sessions and the control group was not.

Findings

Offender attitudes

Offender surveys compared men in the experimental and control groups at time of adjudication, at least 6 months later, and for the change between the two times. By the time of their second interview, 30 percent of the experimental group had concluded their counseling program. More important, the sample as a whole had completed an average of 22 of the 26 mandated counseling sessions (approximately 85 percent of the intended "dosage" of counseling).

Approximately half of the men viewed battering as acceptable in certain situations. No differences were found between the

experimental and control groups in the first or second surveys or over time. There was no difference between groups initially or over time in their views of the proper roles of women, whether battering should be considered a crime, or whether the State had a right to intervene. Both groups also reported the same likelihood of beating their partners again.

The only change noted in all of these comparisons was a small but significant change in men's views of their partners' responsibility for the offense that led them to court. Over time, those in the control group viewed their partners as increasingly responsible. In contrast, in the 6 months after adjudication, those in the experimental group saw the woman as slightly less responsible. Even so, however, the men in the experimental group still viewed their partners as "somewhat" to "equally" responsible for the incident.

Several studies indicate that batterers hold more traditional views than nonbatterers about women and their proper roles. BIPs are based on the premise that teaching men that it is wrong to exert verbal, physical, or sexual control over their partners will lead to changes in their beliefs that will ultimately produce changes in their behavior. The results of these analyses seem to indicate, however, that men directed by courts into BIPs, as compared to men in the control group, did not change their beliefs about the legitimacy of battering, their responsibility for these incidents, and the proper roles for women.

Victim attitudes

Victim interviews clearly indicated that the vast majority of women viewed battering as inappropriate in virtually all contexts. Not surprisingly, this runs counter to what most of the men reported. This held true for victims whose partners were in both groups and did not change over time. Victims reported a more liberal view of

There is no reason to believe that the two groups did not receive the same monitoring, supervision, and treatment throughout the test period, with the exception that the experimental group was required to attend counseling and the control group was not.

women's roles than their partners did. The experimental and control groups showed no differences in women's attitudes about the appropriate role for women, nor did these views change significantly over time.

Victims in both the experimental and control groups shared the same perceptions over time of whether the offense that brought them to court should be viewed as a crime. About 57 percent of the women, compared with 26 percent of the men, believed the offense should be viewed as a crime.

Victims rated themselves as not at all to somewhat responsible for the battering, whereas men rated the women as almost equally responsible. Again, there were no significant differences between the experimental and control groups in women's perceptions of responsibility.

Finally, victims in the experimental and control groups showed no significant differences in their perceptions of the likelihood that their partner would hit them again. This was the case in both the first and second surveys and over time. Women saw such an event as more likely than the men did (20 percent versus 5 percent).

Offender self-reported likelihood to engage in abuse

Thirty percent of the men reported taking what the CTS2 defines as a minor abusive action (including grabbing and slapping) against their partners within 6 months after adjudication. Thirty-two percent of the women reported such an incident within the same period. Eight percent of the men reported engaging in more severe physical abuse (using a knife or gun, choking, or beating up their partner), compared with 14 percent of the women who reported being victims of such abuse.

As exhibit 1 indicates, no differences were found between groups initially or over time in men's self-reported likelihood to engage in any of the activities listed on the CTS2 (negotiation, psychological coercion, physical abuse, sexual coercion, and injury). A regression analysis was performed to determine whether assignment to treatment, treatment received (number of treatment classes attended), or stake-in-conformity variables (e.g., marital status, residential stability, and employment) could account for any differences in men's self-reported use of severe physical violence. Consistent with the analysis of attitudes and beliefs presented above, the results indicated that neither assignment to a BIP nor attending the classes was significant in explaining severe physical violence. Instead, stake-in-conformity variables were important in accounting for this variation. Younger men with no stable residence were significantly more likely to report committing acts of severe physical violence against their partners than their older, more residentially stable counterparts.

Victim reports of their partners' likelihood to engage in abuse

As exhibit 1 indicates, no difference was found between groups or over time in women's reports of their partners' likelihood to engage in any of the activities listed on the CTS2. Fourteen percent of the women reported that an act of severe physical violence occurred during the followup period. Stake-in-conformity variables best predicted repeated battering. Offenders' age and marital status were found to be significant, while offenders' employment, though not significant, demonstrated a strong tendency to relate to victims' reports of severe physical violence. Women involved with, but not married to, younger jobless men were more likely to report incidents of severe physical violence.

Exhibit 1. Revised Conflict Tactics Scale: Average score on scale by survey

Scale	Negotiation		Psychological coercion		Physical coercion		Sexual coercion		Injury	
	Mean Score	N	Mean Score	N	Mean Score	N	Mean Score	N	Mean Score	N
Defendant at sentencing										
Experimental	2.08	153	0.83	155	0.25	143	0.10	154	0.16	159
Control	2.11	117	0.88	117	0.27	115	0.11	113	0.16	123
Defendant at 6 months										
Experimental	1.68	90	0.30	93	0.03	90	0.04	88	0.02	94
Control	1.58	87	0.41	82	0.06	82	0.07	85	0.06	86
Victim at sentencing										
Experimental	1.75	98	1.43	102	0.65	98	0.17	97	0.43	103
Control	1.77	81	1.23	79	0.62	80	0.21	78	0.37	84
Victim at 6 months										
Experimental	1.86	54	1.00	56	0.11	55	0.05	57	0.06	58
Control	1.99	45	0.84	45	0.13	42	0.06	44	0.02	45
Victim at 1 year										
Experimental	1.86	36	0.97	34	0.15	35	0.13	36	0.08	36
Control	1.82	34	0.95	35	0.14	33	0.03	35	0.09	35

Note: Response categories were 0 = never, 1 = 1, 2 = 2–5, 3 = 6+.

Official measures—violations of probation

Comparisons between the experimental and control groups would be unfair if one group could be cited for violations of probation (VOP) for reasons that did not apply to the other group. Men in the experimental group could be held in violation for failing to attend treatment, a probation condition that did not apply to those in the control group. Analysis indicated, however, that although probationers may have had their probations revoked for failing to attend treatment, in all cases but one, this was only one of several reasons listed in the revocation. It does not seem that men were found to be in violation of probation exclusively for failing to attend domestic violence classes.

Forty-eight percent of the experimental group and 45 percent of the men in the control group were cited for VOPs at least once during their year on probation. This difference was not significant. Another regression analysis was performed to determine whether treatment assigned, treatment received, or stake-in-conformity variables could account for the variation. Other things being equal, those assigned to the experimental group were 2.8 times more likely to be cited for VOPs than those in the control group. The more classes a man attended, the less likely he was to be cited for VOPs. That attendance of domestic violence classes was

mandatory, however, somewhat offset their estimated benefit.

The importance of stake-in-conformity variables in predicting successful completion of probation is clear. The number of months employed best predicts VOP. Residential stability, age, and marital status also are significantly related to VOP. A man who moves is more likely to be cited for probation violations, as are younger jobless men. Married men are less likely to be cited for probation violations. This increase in likelihood of violation does not seem to be due to increased monitoring; no significant differences were found between groups in the way the probation office monitored batterers on probation.

Official measures—rearrests

Twenty-four percent of men in both the experimental and control groups were rearrested at least once during their year on probation. Regression analysis was performed to determine whether treatment assigned, treatment received, or stake-in-conformity variables were significant in predicting rearrest. Assignment to the experimental group was not significantly related to likelihood of being rearrested, but attending domestic violence classes and the interaction between group assignment and treatment received were significant in predicting rearrests, as were employment and age. Employment was the most important factor accounting for variation in rearrests. These findings lead to two primary conclusions. First, batterers who are assigned to treatment and fail to attend most or all of the sessions are more likely to be rearrested than similarly situated men who are not ordered to attend counseling. Second, lack of steady employment is more important than nonattendance in predicting rearrest.

Attending domestic violence classes can significantly reduce the likelihood of rearrest both for those assigned to the BIP

and for those placed into the control group. When comparing similarly situated men (in terms of marital status, employment, residential stability, and age), however, those in the control group almost always fared better than those in the experimental group on rearrest.

Design limitations

The controversy surrounding the Broward experiment led to low victim response rates, high staff turnover, delays, and other problems. The low victim response rate was a special concern because research consistently indicates that victims provide the best information on continuing abuse.[7] Despite these concerns, the fact that this study collected information from multiple sources (men's self-reports, victims' reports, and official measures) that all indicated similar conclusions bolstered researchers' confidence in the results from each measure.

This experiment provided a valid and rigorous test of the effectiveness of court-mandated counseling as carried out in Broward County that ought to be performed in other jurisdictions. The authors have been candid in disclosing the problems involved in conducting this study[8] in the hope that others will learn from their mistakes and build better and stronger experiments.

Policy implications

The results of this study show that counseling had no clear and demonstrable effect on offenders' attitudes, beliefs, or behavior. Evidence of severe physical abuse still existed, even at 6 and 12 months after sentencing.

Official reports provided some evidence that men assigned to the counseling programs were more likely to be rearrested than those in the control group unless

The results of this study show that counseling had no clear and demonstrable effect on offenders' attitudes, beliefs, or behavior.

they attended all of the court-mandated counseling sessions. Some may say that this proves that every legal means must be used to get batterers to attend treatment. Even those men who attended all their sessions, however, were only slightly less likely to be rearrested than similarly situated men in the control group who attended no sessions. When they did not attend all the sessions, they were more likely to be rearrested than their counterparts in the control group.

The charge to "throw the book" at the man who does not attend all of his treatment sessions seems to miss the point. In this jurisdiction, unlike those observed by Adele Harrell[9] and Sally Palmer and her colleagues,[10] men were monitored and sanctioned. Although approximately 33 percent of the men failed to attend treatment, all of them were cited for violating one or more probation conditions and 71 percent of them were cited for failing to attend counseling. The probation office did its job; probation was revoked when men did not complete the batterers' program. Nevertheless, some men completed the treatment and others dropped out. Finally, this study indicated the importance of stake-in-conformity variables in predicting rearrest among men convicted of misdemeanor domestic violence.

Notes

1. The terms "convicted" or "adjudicated" have legal significance. This study included men who had either (1) pled guilty or no contest to domestic violence battery charges or who were found guilty after trial and were placed on probation, or (2) been placed on probation, whether adjudicated guilty or not, for the offense of domestic violence battery, or (3) been found guilty of or placed on probation for crimes of domestic violence. The vast majority of defendants (96 percent) pled no contest to the charges. Throughout this report, this entire group of men is referred to as those adjudicated or convicted of a misdemeanor domestic violence charge.

2. $t = 1.42$, $p > .05$.

3. $t = 2.81$, $p < .01$.

4. Edleson, J., Z. Eisikovits, and E. Guttmann, "Men Who Batter Women: A Critical Review of the Evidence," *Journal of Family Issues* 6(2)(1985): 229–247; Hamberger, L.K., and J. Hastings, "Recidivism Following Spouse Abuse Abatement Counseling: Treatment Program Implications," *Violence and Victims* 5(3)(1990): 157–170; Hotaling, G., and D. Sugarman, "An Analysis of Risk Markers in Husband to Wife Violence: The Current State of Knowledge," *Violence and Victims* 1(2)(1986): 101–124.

5. Hirschel, J.D., and I. Hutchinson, "Female Spouse Abuse and the Police Response: The Charlotte, North Carolina Experiment," *Journal of Criminal Law and Criminology* 83(1)(1992): 73–119; Palmer, S., R. Brown, and M. Barrera, "Group Treatment Program for Abusive Husbands: Long-Term Evaluation," *American Journal of Orthopsychiatric Association* 62(2)(1992): 276–283; Tolman, R., and A. Weisz, "Coordinated Community Intervention for Domestic Violence: The Effects of Arrest and Prosecution on Recidivism of Woman Abuse Perpetrators," *Crime and Delinquency* 41(4)(1995): 481–495.

6. Petersilia, J., "Implementing Randomized Experiments: Lessons from BJA's Intensive Supervision Project," *Evaluation Review* 13(5)(1989): 435–458; Babbie, E., *The Practice of Social Research*, Belmont, CA: Wadsworth, 1998.

7. Arias, I., and S. Beach, "Validity of Self-Reports of Marital Violence," *Journal of Family Violence* 2(2)(1987): 139–149; Edleson, J., and M. Brygger, "Gender Differences in Reporting of Battering Incidences," in *Understanding Partner Violence: Prevalence, Causes, Consequences, and Solutions*, ed. S. Stith and M. Straus, Minneapolis, MN: National Council of Family Relations, 1995: 45–50.

8. Feder, L., and D.R. Forde, "A Test of the Efficacy of Court-Mandated Counseling for Domestic Violence Offenders: The Broward Experiment," Final report for National Institute of Justice, grant number 96–WT–NX–0008, Washington, DC: National Institute of Justice, 2000. NCJRS. NCJ 184752.

9. Harrell, A., *Evaluation of Court-Ordered Treatment for Domestic Violence Offenders: Final Report*, Washington, DC: Institute for Social Analysis, 1991.

10. Palmer, S., R. Brown, and M. Barrera, "Group Treatment Program for Abusive Husbands: Long-Term Evaluation."

The Brooklyn Experiment

Robert C. Davis, Christopher D. Maxwell, and Bruce G. Taylor

About the Authors

Robert C. Davis is senior research associate at the Vera Institute of Justice in New York City. Christopher D. Maxwell is an assistant professor at Michigan State University's School of Criminal Justice. Bruce G. Taylor is deputy director of the Arrestee Drug Abuse Monitoring (ADAM) Program in NIJ's Office of Research and Evaluation. At the time this research was conducted, all three were affiliated with Victim Services Research in New York City.

Differences among the studies

Voluntary versus involuntary treatment

Unlike in the Broward County experiment and a similar study by Sally Palmer and her colleagues,[1] batterers in this study were mandated to treatment by judicial order rather than probation departments. This difference has implications for the kinds of batterers studied. The Palmer and Broward County studies included all or most batterers sentenced to probation, whether or not they were willing to undergo treatment. In this study, batterers were eligible for inclusion only if all parties to the case (prosecution, defense, and judge) agreed treatment was appropriate. In several cases, such agreement could not be reached, usually because the defense refused to agree to treatment. Thus, the results of this study are harder to generalize than the results of the Palmer and Broward County experiments. On the other hand, because all batterers in this study's sample agreed to treatment, the study presumably did not include unmotivated batterers.[2] This point is crucial because it has often been argued that treatment cannot be expected to work for individuals who are compelled to attend against their will.[3]

Control group differences

This difference in how batterers were mandated to treatment also has implications for comparison groups. The Palmer and Broward County studies compared treatment with no treatment. In contrast, this study compares batterers assigned to treatment with batterers assigned to a community service program irrelevant to the problem of violence. The comparison between batterer treatment and an irrelevant treatment is appropriate for judicially mandated treatment referrals (since all convicted batterers must receive some sentence), just as the comparison between treatment and no treatment is appropriate for probation-mandated referrals.

Differences in length of treatment

As described in detail below, the treatment sample in this study was split into two subsamples. Although all batterers randomly assigned to treatment were ordered to attend 39 hours of group treatment based on the Duluth model, some attended 1.5-hour weekly sessions for 26 weeks, while others attended 2.5-hour sessions twice a week for 8 weeks. The former treatment model maximized the time batterers stayed in treatment; the latter reduced the chances that batterers' initial motivation to seek treatment would flag over time.

Methodology

In this study, which was conducted using a true experimental design, 376 criminal court defendants were mandated to attend a 39-hour batterer treatment program or complete 39 hours of community service. Random assignment was made at sentencing after all parties (judge, prosecutor, and defense) had agreed to accept a random assignment to batterer treatment.

Batterers and victims were interviewed about new violence on three occasions: at sentencing, 6 months later, and 12 months later. Official data on new complaints to the police and new arrests were gathered at 6 and 12 months after sentencing.

Cases included

The sampling frame consisted of spousal assault cases in Kings County (Brooklyn, New York) Criminal Court. All parties agreed in principle to accept batterer treatment if the defendant was accepted by the Alternatives to Violence (ATV) program. Selection began on February 19, 1995, and ran through March 1, 1996. During that time, 376 cases were taken into the sample, a small percentage of the cases adjudicated during the selection period.

In 64 percent of the cases in the study, defendants were charged with third-degree assault (a class A misdemeanor). Another 19 percent were charged with felonious assault (although they pleaded to misdemeanor charges). The remaining 17 percent were charged with violating restraining orders, menacing, harassment, and other offenses. Defendants most commonly pleaded guilty and were then given a conditional discharge that placed them under court control for 1 year. Twenty-three percent of the cases were adjourned in contemplation of dismissal (cases would be dismissed and records expunged if defendants avoided arrest and adhered to judicial conditions for 6 months).

The ATV curriculum

ATV was based on the Duluth model, which assumes that domestic violence is a byproduct of male and female roles that result in an imbalance of power. The curriculum included defining domestic violence, understanding the historical and cultural aspects of domestic abuse, and reviewing criminal and legal issues. Through a combination of instruction and discussion, participants were encouraged to take responsibility for their anger, actions, and reactions. Sessions were conducted in English and Spanish by two leaders, one male and one female.

Selection difficulties

At the time the experiment began, ATV had just expanded the number of required hours from 1.5 hours once a week for 12 weeks to 1.5 hours once a week for 26 weeks. This was done to conform with New York State guidelines and national trends. The longer program, however, drew objections from Legal Aid Society attorneys,[4] who defended most indigent defendants in King County Criminal Court. The attorneys began to advise their clients against involvement in the program. Selection slowed to a standstill. At a meeting with the attorneys, it became clear that they objected to the increased time their clients would be under court control and the higher session fees they would have to pay over the course of 26 sessions.

If selection was to be completed on time, these objections would have to be accommodated. ATV administrators designed a new 8-week format, through which participants could complete the same 39 hours of treatment in twice-weekly, 2.5-hour sessions with lower fees per session. The new format began to be offered after the first 129 participants had been assigned to 26-week groups. From August 15, 1995, until selection was completed, defendants were offered a choice between 8-week and 26-week formats. Once the 8-week groups became available, none of the final 61 participants chose the 26-week option.

Control group

Defendants selected by lottery to the control group were mandated by judges to participate in 39 hours of community

service, typically over 2 weeks. For offenders with jobs, flexible hours were arranged over a 2-month period so they could continue their jobs. Participants renovated housing units, cleared vacant lots to make way for community gardens, painted senior-citizen centers, and cleaned up playgrounds—all activities that would be expected to have little effect on abusive behavior. During their service, participants were educated about drugs and HIV. Interested individuals were referred to drug, HIV, or employment counseling programs.

Participants in both batterer treatment and community service programs were expelled if a pattern of nonattendance developed (for ATV, three misses constituted grounds for expulsion). For men assigned to batterer treatment, such cases were referred to the District Attorney's Office. At the prosecutor's discretion, delinquent cases could be returned to the court calendar and new sentences imposed. In practice, however, few cases were restored to the calendar because the period of court supervision typically was drawing to a close by the time a clear pattern of noncompliance was established and a request for restoration completed.

Followup on delinquents was more reliable for the community service group. The organization running the program had the authority to place delinquent cases on the court calendar itself, rather than recommending that the prosecutor do so. If the court issued an arrest warrant for noncompliance, the community service program had enforcement staff to execute the warrants.

Assignment process

Cases were drawn from three of eight postarraignment courts in Kings County Criminal Court. Two of the courts were specialized domestic violence courts. The third was a jury trial court where domestic violence cases were transferred if a disposition could not be negotiated. When

judge, prosecutor, and defense reached agreement on batterer treatment as an appropriate disposition, defendants were screened by ATV for eligibility and assigned by lottery to batterer treatment or community service.

After assignment to treatment, the defendant was accompanied back to the courtroom and the prosecutor was told of the lottery assignment. The prosecutor told the judge, who then accepted a disposition consistent with the assignment. In 28 percent of the cases in which batterers were randomly assigned to the control program, judges mandated that batterers receive treatment instead. Judges overrode no cases randomly assigned to the ATV program.

Followup measures

The most important test of effectiveness for any batterer treatment program is whether it reduces violence. Therefore, this study included both short-term (6 months after sentencing) and intermediate-term (12 months after sentencing) followup on treatment outcomes. Short-term outcomes are important to assess because any treatment effects may be short-lived. The more time passes after a domestic complaint to police, the less likely future violence becomes.[5] Any early differences in violence due to treatment might disappear as violence in the control group declines over time. Longer term followup is important to determine whether short-term treatment effects continue after batterers are no longer attending treatment or under court control.

The study included two measures of new batterer-victim violence: new incidents reported to criminal justice authorities involving the same victim and victim reports of new incidents to research interviewers.[6] Violence indicators do not always behave in similar ways,[7] so it is important to capture more than one. Both measures were captured at 6 and 12

The most important test for any batterer treatment program is whether it reduces violence.

months after sentencing. Crime report and arrest data were obtained from official records. Victim self-reports were obtained primarily through telephone interviews.

In addition to capturing information on new violent acts, the interviews assessed attitudes and cognitive behaviors among batterers and victims. Conflict resolution skills and attitudes toward violence in the family were measured for both the treatment and control groups. Batterers and victims were tested to see whether they believed they could influence events or thought things simply happened to them.[8] It seemed plausible to assume that, if batterer treatment succeeded in making batterers take more responsibility for their actions, their test results would show more control over those actions. Victims were tested to see how well they were adjusting psychologically. If post-treatment tests showed that victims had higher self-esteem and a greater sense of well-being, it could be a sign that treatment had produced a change in the way batterers treated their partners.

Interview methodology

Researchers tried to interview defendants and victims on three occasions: at selection (court disposition), 6 months later, and 12 months later. Batterers were interviewed in person in the court building just before they were assigned to batterer treatment or community service. Subsequent interviews with batterers and all interviews with victims were conducted primarily by telephone. Because it was believed victims would be more truthful than batterers in talking about new violence, special efforts were put into interviewing victims. When telephone attempts failed, teams of interviewers were sent to victims' homes. If these attempts also failed, letters were mailed offering first $25 and then $50 for completion of an interview. In the third set of victim interviews, 70 difficult cases were turned over to a licensed private investigator. The investigator used databases to track victims who had moved and provided the research team with current addresses. He did not confront victims or their acquaintances. The research team tried to interview women he located by telephone. Ultimately, however, this additional tracking led to no more interviews.

Completion rates

The completion rate for victim interviews was 50 percent for the first interview, 46 percent for the second, and 50 percent for the third. First interviews with batterers were obtained with 95 percent of the sample when defendants were present in court for selection to the treatment program. For the second and third interviews, completion rates were 40 and 24 percent. Completion rates were substantially higher for victim interviews because researchers went to extra lengths (incentives, in-person visits) to obtain them.

Findings

Treatment effects on behavior

Initial analyses showed that batterers assigned to treatment were less likely to be accused of battering the same victim again than batterers assigned to

Exhibit 1. Prevalence of criminal justice incidents involving the same victim and perpetrator

	6 months after assignment*	12 months after assignment**
Batterer treatment (n = 190)	10%	15%
Community service (n = 186)	22%	26%

* *Chi*-square (1) = 10.43, *p* = .001
** *Chi*-square (1) = 7.78, *p* = .005

community service. This difference was most pronounced at 6 months after group assignment, but persisted for a full year (see exhibit 1).

Batterers were far more likely to complete the shorter course of treatment. Roughly similar proportions of batterers began treatment in both groups (77 percent of those assigned to the 8-week group and 71 percent of those assigned to the 26-week group attended at least one class), but 67 percent of the men assigned to the 8-week group graduated, compared with just 27 percent of those assigned to the 26-week group (see exhibit 2).[9]

Researchers expected that men assigned to the 8-week group would have a lower reoffense rate than men assigned to the 26-week group because a larger proportion of them completed the program. Only the 26-week group, however, had significantly fewer criminal complaints than the control group at 6 and 12 months after sentencing: The 8-week group and the control group were virtually indistinguishable (see exhibit 3).

Victim reports of violence also showed that men who attended 26 weeks of treatment committed fewer new violent acts than those who attended 8 weeks or no treatment. These differences, however, were not statistically significant (see exhibit 4).

Even when defendants' age, ethnicity, marital status, employment status, and arrest history were factored in, the 26-week group had fewer complaints of new crimes against their battering victims than the 8-week and control groups. In addition, reports of criminal complaints showed that those in the 26-week group went significantly longer before battering again.[10]

Treatment effects on attitudes

Researchers also looked at measures of cognitive change in batterers, including conflict resolution skills, beliefs about domestic violence, and internal versus external control. As shown in exhibit 5, there is no basis for claiming that treatment changed batterers' attitudes or ways of dealing with conflict.[11]

Exhibit 2. Attendance in 8- versus 26-week batterers' group

	No attendance	Some attendance	Graduated
26-week format (n = 129)	29%	44%	27%
8-week format (n = 61)	23%	10%	67%

Exhibit 3. Prevalence of criminal justice incidents involving same victim and perpetrator

	6 months after assignment*	12 months after assignment**
26-week batterer treatment (n = 129)	7%	10%
8-week batterer treatment (n = 61)	15%	25%
Control (community service) (n = 186)	22%	26%

* Chi-square (2) = 12.35, p = .003
** Chi-square (2) = 13.13, p = .001

Exhibit 4. Prevalence of incidents reported by victims to research interviewers

	6 months after assignment*	12 months after assignment*
26-week batterer treatment	23% (n = 52)	14% (n = 66)
8-week batterer treatment	19% (n = 26)	18% (n = 33)
Control (community service)	21% (n = 93)	22% (n = 90)

* Chi-square (2) = 0.15, p = .926
** Chi-square (2) = 1.86, p = .394

Exhibit 5. Means and standard deviations for psychosocial outcomes

		Control (n = 69)		8-week (n = 27)		26-week (n = 53)		
		Mean	Std. dev.	Mean	Std. dev.	Mean	Std. dev.	F test
6-month survey	Conflict resolution skills	18.1	6.3	19.6	6.1	18.0	5.7	F(2,116)=0.57
	Attitudes toward spouse abuse	25.2	5.5	25.2	6.5	25.2	5.1	F(2,146)=0.00
	Internal/external locus of control	3.5	2.0	2.9	2.4	3.2	2.1	F(2,146)=0.41
12-month survey	Conflict resolution skills	19.3	6.2	19.1	6.0	19.9	5.9	F(2,62)=0.91
	Attitudes toward spouse abuse	24.4	4.1	25.1	4.8	25.9	4.6	F(2,85)=0.35
	Internal/external locus of control	3.5	2.0	3.1	2.5	3.1	2.1	F(2,85)=0.51

Design limitations

This study illustrates the difficulties that can be encountered in carrying out an experiment with a true experimental design. Substantial concessions had to be made to court officials to gain their cooperation. Judges were allowed to override assignments to the control group. If override cases had been included in the control group, the tests of treatment effects would have been made more conservative. (Nonetheless, large treatment effects were still found.) Also, the research team had to offer a treatment alternative that was more palatable to the defense than the lengthy and costly version it started with. This proved to be fortuitous because substantial differences in outcomes were found between men assigned to the 8-week and 26-week groups.

Policy implications

Does batterer intervention modify attitudes and behavior in a relatively lasting way, or does it simply suppress violent behavior for the duration of treatment? The results of this study do not support the view that treatment leads to lasting changes in behavior. Were that true, the men in the 8-week group (who finished their treatment long before the followup period expired) ought to have been no more violent than their counterparts in the 26-week program (who were in treatment for most of the followup period). That is not what this study showed. Nor was any evidence found that treatment altered batterers' attitudes toward spouse abuse, which further suggests that treatment brought about no permanent changes.

The results of this study thus support the view that batterer intervention merely suppresses violent behavior for the duration of treatment. Since, however, the study was not designed to test the validity of various treatment models, the results cannot be seen as conclusive. Moreover, they are at odds with results of other studies that found no difference in reoffense rates according to length of treatment.[12] Many batterer programs are adopting longer

treatment models, but there is substantial pressure from the defense bar and economics to keep time in treatment to a minimum. Thus, the question of whether treatment works only as long as men attend counseling is crucial to intelligent policy formulation.

Notes

1. Palmer, S.E., R.A. Brown, and M.E. Barrera, "Group Treatment Program for Abusive Husbands: Long-Term Evaluation," *American Journal of Orthopsychiatry* 62(2)(1992): 276–283; Feder, L., and D.R. Forde, "A Test of the Efficacy of Court-Mandated Counseling for Domestic Violence Offenders: The Broward Experiment," Final Report for the National Institute of Justice, grant number 96–WT–NX–008, Washington, DC: National Institute of Justice, 2000. NCJRS. NCJ 184752.

2. Of course, participants did not seek treatment of their own volition; they were mandated by the court to do so. Still, it is common knowledge in Brooklyn Criminal Court that misdemeanor batterer defendants are not facing jail time. Participants in treatment certainly knew from counsel that they were choosing the batterer program not as the only way to keep out of jail but over another alternative to incarceration.

3. Rosenfeld, B.D., "Court-Ordered Treatment of Spouse Abuse," *Clinical Psychology Review* 12(1992): 205–226.

4. At the time the change was made, Legal Aid administrators had pledged cooperation and had made good on that pledge.

5. Davis, R.C., and B.G. Taylor, "A Proactive Response to Family Violence: The Results of a Randomized Experiment," *Criminology* 35(2)(1997): 307–333.

6. These indicators are commonly used in studies tracking households where domestic violence occurs, such as NIJ's Spouse Assault Replication Program research. See, for example, Fagan, J., J. Garner, and C.D. Maxwell, "Reducing Injuries to Women in Domestic Assaults," Final Report, Washington DC: U.S. Department of Health and Human Services, Centers for Disease Control and Prevention, National Center for Injury Control and Prevention, 1997.

7. See, for example, Davis, R.C. and B.G. Taylor, "A Proactive Response to Family Violence: The Results of a Randomized Experiment."

8. Cognitive measures included the Inventory of Beliefs About Wife Beating Scale, Harrell's measure of Conflict Resolution Skills, and a shortened (12-item) version of the Nowicki-Strickland Internal-External Control Scale. Saunders, D.G., A.B. Lynch, M. Grayson, and D. Linz, "Inventory of Beliefs about Wife Beating: The Construction and Initial Validation of a Measure of Beliefs and Attitudes," *Violence and Victims* (2) (1987): 39–55; Harrell, A., *Evaluation of Court-Ordered Treatment for Domestic Violence Offencers,* Final Report to the State Justice Institute, Washington, DC: The Urban Institute, 1991; Nowicki, S., and M.P. Duke, "A Locus of Control Scale for Non-College as Well as College Adults," *Journal of Personality Assessment* 38 (1974): 136–137.

9. *Chi*-square (1) = 27.72, $p < .001$.

10. See Davis, R.C., B.G. Taylor, and C.D. Maxwell, "Does Batterer Treatment Reduce Violence? A Randomized Experiment in Brooklyn—Executive Summary Included," Final Report for National Institute of Justice, grant 94–IJ–CX–0047. Washington DC: National Institute of Justice, 2000. NCJRS. NCJ 180772.

11. For each scale, means across the three treatment groups are remarkably similar, and none of the tests shown in exhibit 5 comes close to statistical significance. Limitations in the scales and the data, however, do not permit a complete test of this hypothesis. For a discussion of these limitations, the reader is referred to the full report. See Davis, R.C., B.G. Taylor, and C.D. Maxwell, "Does Batterer Treatment Reduce Violence? A Randomized Experiment in Brooklyn—Executive Summary Included."

12. Edleson, J.L., and M. Syers, "Relative Effectiveness of Group Treatments for Men Who Batter," *Social Work Research and Abstracts* 26(2) (1989): 10–17; Gondolf, E., *Multi-Site Evaluation of Batterer Intervention Systems: A Summary of Preliminary Findings* (Indiana, PA: Mid-Atlantic Addiction Training Institute, 1997).

Analyzing the Studies

Shelly Jackson

There are two possible explanations for the finding that the batterer intervention programs (BIPs) in Brooklyn and Broward County had little or no effect on their clients. One is that the evaluations were methodologically flawed; the other is that design of the programs themselves may be flawed. These two explanations are not necessarily mutually exclusive.

Methodological issues

Response and attrition rates

Both programs had low response rates and high dropout rates[1]—characteristics that can lead to overly positive estimates of program effects. Those who continue to batter are not likely to participate in intervention programs; if they participate in the beginning, they are likely to drop out. Hence, drawing on a sample of "available" participants is problematic. It is unclear whether the effect found in the Brooklyn evaluation is the result of attrition or a true program or monitoring effect.

About the Author

Shelly Jackson is a program manager in NIJ's Office of Research and Evaluation.

Valid and reliable outcome measures

Another problem that complicates BIP evaluations is the lack of valid and reliable measures of batterer behavior and attitudes. The revised Conflict Tactics Scale (CTS2) is often used, but this instrument was not designed to be repeated over time. It therefore may be an inappropriate tool for "before" and "after" measurements. Because no scientifically agreed-

upon outcome measures exist specifically for this purpose, at a minimum, evaluations should include multiple outcome instruments that use multiple sources to validate results.[2]

Multiple sources of data

Using more than one source of data to measure the impact of a program increases the validity of the findings. Both studies used multiple data sources (batterer self-reports, victim reports, and official records). In Brooklyn, the researchers initially found differences only in batterers' reports of battering again. After statistically controlling for several variables, however, victim reports and official records replicated those reports. Although official records commonly are used to validate batterer and victim reports, the use of official rearrest records remains problematic. Rearrests capture only those violations that reach the authorities, whereas there is evidence that batterers often avoid rearrest by using psychological and verbal abuse.[3] Probation violations, another form of official records used in the Broward County study, are likely to be overly broad and may not necessarily indicate a battering incident.

Definition of success

A related issue is whether success should be defined as complete cessation of violence or merely as a reduction in violence.[4] The studies in this report consider a reduction in violence to be a success. This choice is based on the premise that it

may be unrealistic to expect batterers to change an established pattern of behavior dramatically after a relatively short intervention. Yet even a statistically significant reduction in violence may be of little practical significance to a battered woman.[5]

Problems with random assignment

Ensuring that assignment is truly random is often difficult.

Random assignment to treatment and control groups is critical in an experimental study. It makes certain that preexisting differences between the groups are evenly distributed and allows researchers to conclude that the program is responsible for any subsequent differences. Ensuring that assignment is truly random, however, is often difficult.

In Broward County, changes to random assignment were minimal. The Brooklyn study experienced considerably more difficulty in this respect. After agreement of the courts had already been obtained, the length of the intervention had to be increased from 12 to 26 weeks to comply with New York State guidelines. This change apparently concerned many defense attorneys. After the evaluation had already begun (129 subjects had been enrolled in the 26-week evaluation), the Legal Aid Society, which represented many of the defendants, began to advise its clients not to participate. Research assignment to the intervention ceased. To obtain the necessary number of clients in the research sample, a compromise was reached: An 8-week program was offered that contained the same content as the 26-week program. All batterers assigned to treatment thereafter chose the 8-week program. Allowing batterers to choose between treatment programs poses a problem because there can be no assurance that the group of defendants who chose the 8-week program was not systematically different from the group

assigned to the 26-week program. Thus, effects cannot be attributed exclusively to the program (i.e., alternative explanations are plausible). Moreover, in 28 percent of the control cases in the Brooklyn evaluation, judges overrode the random assignment and mandated that batterers receive treatment (these cases were appropriately included in the analyses). In addition, some participants in both versions of the program were expelled for repeated nonattendance.

These compromises in random assignment dilute the potential impact of the intervention and seriously limit the ability to generalize about the evaluation results. Although the integrity of the Broward County experiment's random assignment was better, even there, judges overrode the random assignment in 3.5 percent of the cases. Each compromise of the random assignment decreases confidence in the results.

Attendance problems

Many batterers did not attend some or all of their treatment sessions; in Broward County, 13 percent of the treatment group attended no classes at all and 3 percent of the control group attended some classes. This raises another serious methodological issue: What is being measured, treatment assignment or treatment effects? If batterers can choose to complete or drop out of treatment, the strength of the experimental design is compromised. Thus, it can be argued that these evaluations were examining the effects of assignment to a treatment group as much as the effects of the intervention itself, because not everyone in the treatment group received the entire intervention. Feder and Forde statistically tested for this possibility and found no treatment effects. Nonetheless, this is a common problem BIP evaluations have to face.

Time of offense

Until recently, evaluation researchers have not considered the time of offense when measuring outcomes. Yet this is important to know. If the offender batters again during the first week of treatment, it cannot be said that the program had no effect; rather, the program had no opportunity to affect the batterer. In contrast, if the offender batters again near the end of the intervention or later, that may better indicate program effectiveness. Davis, Taylor, and Maxwell analyzed the Brooklyn data to control for this possibility. Feder and Forde, however, did not consider time of offense in Broward County, which makes it more difficult to interpret their results.

Program design issues

In addition to these methodological problems, problems with the design of BIPs themselves could limit their effectiveness.

Faithfulness to program model

Program models are sometimes not carried out completely. Testing how faithful programs are to the models on which they are based requires process evaluations, which, to date, few evaluations have incorporated.

Conceptual limitations

BIP designs also may have conceptual limitations. The Duluth model assumes that all batterers seek to control their partners. Batterers' motivations for violence may differ, so the same type of intervention may not work with all batterers.

BIPs also may be limited by their lack of cultural specificity.[6] Although domestic violence occurs in all populations, treatment approaches may need to be tailored to serve specific populations. It may be unreasonable to expect Duluth-model interventions based on white feminist theory to work effectively with minority populations. Not everyone agrees with this proposition, however. The House of Ruth in Baltimore, Maryland, deliberately created an ethnically integrated group treatment setting based on the Duluth model to stress that domestic violence has nothing to do with race or socioeconomic status. NIJ has recently funded an experimental evaluation to examine whether a batterer intervention model designed specifically for black men is more effective for them than an integrated model.

Accommodating special needs

Although this is changing, few interventions to date have assessed abusers' mental health and substance abuse treatment needs. These factors do not excuse the battering, but they may make interventions less effective. Including more services, however, may have the unintended effect of increasing the length of a program, its associated costs, and possibly its dropout rates. It is unclear which is more effective: keeping program length to a minimum or adding components (and thereby lengthening the program). These factors deserve more research.

Willingness to change

Programs may remain minimally effective until they consider the batterer's readiness to change. Theories focusing on understanding the stages of personal change suggest that the batterer will change his behavior only when he is ready to change.[7] Thus, mandating treatment for batterers who are not ready to change may be ineffective. BIPs may be effective for batterers who are ready to change, but batterers who are not yet ready may require other interventions.

Problems with the design of batterer intervention programs could limit their effectiveness.

The stakes for women's safety are simply too high to rely on batterer intervention programs without stronger empirical evidence that they work.

Policy implications and future directions

Although interventions are proliferating, there is little evidence that they work. This raises important policy questions:

- Do batterer intervention programs waste valuable resources?

- Do they create a false sense of security in women who are led to believe that their batterer will reform?

- Is it prudent to mandate batterers to BIPs when there is little evidence that they work?

Unfortunately, the latest contributions to this growing literature cannot answer these questions and raise additional issues. Although the Brooklyn study found some differences between those who completed the 8-week program, those who completed the 26-week program, and those who attended no program, it remains unclear whether these differences were due to a program effect or a monitoring effect. Further research is needed to clarify this issue.

One thing is clear: Rigorous evaluations are essential to answering the pressing questions about what works and using that knowledge to influence public policy. The stakes for women's safety are simply too high to rely heavily on the use of BIPs without stronger empirical evidence that they work.

Are these evaluations accurate in saying that BIPs are not very effective at changing batterers' behaviors and attitudes, or are the small program effects merely the result of methodological shortcomings in the evaluations themselves that mask program effectiveness? Both issues may

need to be addressed. To enhance our knowledge, both BIPs and evaluations likely will have to be improved.

Improving program evaluations

Over the years, the quality of BIP evaluation has improved steadily,[8] but several barriers remain to be addressed. Although a variety of designs have been used to study BIPs (e.g., pre-post, quasi-experimental, and experimental designs), most researchers still consider the experiment to be the best evaluation method. Experimental designs are difficult to carry out in court settings; the pressures involved reduce many experimental evaluations to quasi-experiments that cannot deliver the necessary knowledge. Researchers, practitioners, and policymakers must work together to develop strategies that enable experimental evaluations to be carried out vigorously. All BIP evaluations, regardless of design, face difficulties in interviewing batterers and victims during the followup period. Researchers will need to find innovative ways to maintain contact with batterers and victims over time.[9] Researchers also will need to develop reliable and valid outcome measures rather than relying solely on official records such as rearrests and probation violations to validate batterer and victim reports.

Statistical tools can be used to enhance evaluation results once an experimental evaluation has been completed. One tool is selection modeling,[10] which can account for nonrandom assignment. The bootstrap method, which provides a simple means for obtaining an approximate sampling distribution of the statistic that is conditional on the observed data, is another.[11] Survival or event history analyses may be useful in accounting for outcomes over time.[12] By undertaking reviews of several studies, researchers

may be able to aggregate small-scale studies that may have insufficient power to detect differences on their own.[13]

Improving intervention programs

In addition to improving the quality of the experimental design and results, improvements in the concepts underlying the various models of BIPs may be warranted. New intervention approaches could be developed based on theories derived from existing research into the causes of battering.[14] Useful research has been conducted on batterer profiles, and new treatment approaches are being designed to match those profiles with appropriate interventions.[15] Although this approach still must be tested, it may prove more productive than a one-size-fits-all approach. It also may be advantageous for researchers to draw lessons from other disciplines, such as substance abuse interventions.

BIPs may be effective only in the context of broader criminal justice innovations. It may be helpful to see interventions as part of a broader criminal justice and community response to domestic violence that includes arrest, restraining orders, intensive monitoring of batterers,[16] and changes to social norms that may inadvertently tolerate partner violence. If monitoring is in part responsible for lower reoffense rates, as the Brooklyn experiment suggests, judicial monitoring may be particularly effective.[17] The Judicial Oversight Demonstration initiative, a collaboration of NIJ, the Violence Against Women Office, and three local jurisdictions, is testing this proposition.[18] Other innovations might include mandatory intervention until a committee determines that the batterer is no longer a danger to his partner (i.e., indeterminate

probation and intervention), an approach that has been used with sex offenders.[19]

Improvements in the ways BIPs are put into practice may also be necessary, as variations in how programs are carried out may reduce program effectiveness. Some programs have few sanctions for dropping out, whereas others closely monitor batterer attendance. This suggests the need to test the effectiveness of close monitoring and required attendance. Consistent with dose-response theory,[20] batterers should be exposed to the entire program before outcome measures are taken. Drug treatment research has shown that length of treatment (i.e., dosage) influences the outcome.[21] One way to determine whether a program is being carried out as designed is to conduct process and impact evaluations at the same time to understand how program implementation affects the impact evaluation.[22]

The field of batterer intervention is still in its infancy, and much remains to be learned. Rather than asking whether BIPs work, a more productive question may be which programs work best for which batterers under which circumstances,[23] a decidedly more complex question. If this approach is adopted, improved theories of batterering will need to precede new responses that will need to be tested. If differential sentencing is incorporated into the criminal justice system, procedures will need to be developed to ensure that it is carried out fairly. As BIPs are a relatively new response to a critical social problem, it is too early to abandon the concept. It is also too early to believe that we have all the answers. Research and evaluation supported by NIJ will continue to add to our growing knowledge of responses to battering, including batterer intervention programs.

It is too early to abandon the concept. It is also too early to believe that we have all the answers.

Notes

1. Feder and Forde: Interviews were conducted with 80 percent of defendants for the initial interview and 50 percent for the second interview; 49 percent of victims for the initial interview, 30 percent and 22 percent for subsequent interviews. Davis, Taylor, and Maxwell: Interviews were conducted with 50 percent of the victims at the first interview, 46 percent and 50 percent for subsequent interviews. Because interviews were conducted in court at intake, 95 percent of batterers were interviewed at adjudication; 40 percent and 24 percent for subsequent interviews.

2. Heckert D.A., and E.W. Gondolf, "Assessing Patterns of Agreement on Assault Among Batterer Program Participants and their Partners," paper presented at the 5th International Family Violence Research Conference at the University of New Hampshire, Durham, NH, June 29–July 2, 1997. Also see Burt, M.R., A.V. Harrell, L.C. Newmark, L.Y. Aron, L.K. Jacobs, et al. *Evaluation Guidebook for Projects Funded by S.T.O.P. Formula Grants Under the Violence Against Women Act,* Washington, DC: The Urban Institute, 1997.

3. Gondolf, E.W., "Patterns of Reassault in Batterer Programs," Violence and Victims 12(4): 373–87; Harrell, A.V., *Evaluation of Court-Ordered Treatment for Domestic Violence Offenders,* Final Report Submitted to the State Justice Institute. Washington, DC: The Urban Institute, 1991.

4. Edleson, J.L., "Controversy and Change in Batterer's Programs," in *Future Interventions with Battered Women and their Families,* ed. J.L. Edleson and Z.C. Eisikovitz. Thousand Oaks, CA: Sage Publications, 1996.

5. Ibid.

6. Williams, O.J., and R.L. Becker, "Domestic Partner Abuse Treatment Programs and Cultural Competence: The Results of a National Survey," *Violence and Victims* 9(3)(1994): 292.

7. Daniels, J.W., and C.M. Murphy, "Stages and Processes of Change in Batterers' Treatment," *Cognitive and Behavioral Practice* 4 (1997): 123–45; Fawcett, G., L.L. Heise, L. Espegel, and S. Pick, "Changing Community Responses to Wife Abuse: A Research and Demonstration Project in Iztacalco, Mexico," *American Psychologist* 54(1999): 41–49; Murphy, C.M., and V.A. Baxter, "Motivating Batterers to Change in the Treatment Context," *Journal of Interpersonal Violence* 12(1997): 417–422.

8. Davis, R.C., and B.G. Taylor, "Does Batterer Treatment Reduce Violence? A Synthesis of the Literature," *Women and Criminal Justice* 10(2)(1999): 69–93.

9. Gondolf, E.W., "Batterer Programs: What We Know and Need to Know," *Journal of Interpersonal Violence* 12(1)(1997): 83–98; Sullivan, C.M., M.H. Rumptz, R. Campbell, K.K. Eby, and W.S. Davidson, "Retaining Participants in Longitudinal Community Research: A Comprehensive Protocol," *Journal of Applied Behavioral Science* 32(3)(1996): 262–76.

10. Gondolf, E.W., and A.S. Jones, "The Program Effect of Batterer Programs in Three Cities," *American Journal of Community Psychology,* June 2000, under review; Rossi, P.H., H.E. Freeman, and M.W. Lipsey, *Evaluation: A Systematic Approach,* 6th ed. Thousand Oaks, CA: Sage Publications, 1999.

11. Fagan, J. *The Criminalization of Domestic Violence: Promises and Limits.* Research Report. Washington, DC: U.S. Department of Justice, National Institute of Justice, January 1996. NCJ 157641.

12. Gondolf, E.W., "Batterer Programs: What We Know and Need to Know."

13. Lipsey, M., G. Chapman, and N. Landenberger, "Cognitive-Behavioral Programs for Offenders: A Synthesis of the Research on their Effectiveness for Reducing Recidivism," paper presented at the "Systematic Reviews of Criminological Interventions" conference, Washington, DC, April 2–3, 2001.

14. Healey, K., C. Smith, and C. O'Sullivan, *Batterer Intervention: Program Approaches and Criminal Justice Strategies,* Issues and Practices, Washington, DC: U.S. Department of Justice, National Institute of Justice, February 1998. NCJ 168638.

For examples of research into the causes of battering, see Moffitt, T.E., and A. Caspi, *Findings About Partner Violence from the Dunedin Multidisciplinary Health and Development Study,* Research in Brief, Washington, DC: U.S. Department of Justice, National Institute of Justice, July 1999. NCJ 170018.

15. Holtzworth-Munroe, A., and G.L. Stuart, "Typologies of Male Batterers: Three Subtypes and the Differences Among Them," *Psychological Bulletin* 116(3)(1994): 476–97; Wexler, D.B., "The Broken Mirror: A Self Psychological Treatment Perspective for Relationship Violence," *Journal of Psychotherapy, Practice, and Research* 8(2)(1999): 129–141.

16. A. Klein, as cited in Healey, K., C. Smith, and C. O'Sullivan, *Batterer Intervention: Program Approaches and Criminal Justice Strategies,* Issues and Practices Washington, DC: U.S. Department of Justice, National Institute of Justice, February 1998. NCJ 168638, p. 10.

17. But see Gondolf, E.W., "Patterns of Reassault in Batterer Programs," *Violence and Victims* 12(4)(1997): 373–87.

18. "Experiment Demonstrates How to Hold Batterers Accountable," *National Institute of Justice Journal* 244 (July 2000): 29.

19. Hafemeister, T.L., "Legal Aspects of the Treatment of Offenders With Mental Disorders," in R.M. Wettstein, ed., *Treatment of Offenders With Mental Disorders* New York: Guilford Press, 1998: 44–125.

20. Howard, K.I., K. Moras, and W. Lutz, "Evaluation of Psychotherapy: Efficacy, Effectiveness, and Patient Progress," *American Psychologist* 51(10)(1996): 1059–1064.

21. Taxman, F.S., "12 Steps to Improved Offender Outcomes: Developing Responsive Systems of Care for Substance-Abusing Offenders," *Corrections Today* 60(6)(1998): 114–117, 166.

22. Rossi, P.H., H.E. Freeman, and M.W. Lipsey, *Evaluation: A Systematic Approach.*

23. Gondolf, E.W., "Batterer Programs: What We Know and Need to Know."

About the National Institute of Justice

NIJ is the research, development, and evaluation agency of the U.S. Department of Justice. The Institute provides objective, independent, evidence-based knowledge and tools to enhance the administration of justice and public safety. NIJ's principal authorities are derived from the Omnibus Crime Control and Safe Streets Act of 1968, as amended (see 42 U.S.C. §§ 3721–3723).

The NIJ Director is appointed by the President and confirmed by the Senate. The Director establishes the Institute's objectives, guided by the priorities of the Office of Justice Programs, the U.S. Department of Justice, and the needs of the field. The Institute actively solicits the views of criminal justice and other professionals and researchers to inform its search for the knowledge and tools to guide policy and practice.

Strategic Goals

NIJ has seven strategic goals grouped into three categories:

Creating relevant knowledge and tools

1. Partner with State and local practitioners and policymakers to identify social science research and technology needs.
2. Create scientific, relevant, and reliable knowledge—with a particular emphasis on terrorism, violent crime, drugs and crime, cost-effectiveness, and community-based efforts—to enhance the administration of justice and public safety.
3. Develop affordable and effective tools and technologies to enhance the administration of justice and public safety.

Dissemination

4. Disseminate relevant knowledge and information to practitioners and policymakers in an understandable, timely, and concise manner.
5. Act as an honest broker to identify the information, tools, and technologies that respond to the needs of stakeholders.

Agency management

6. Practice fairness and openness in the research and development process.
7. Ensure professionalism, excellence, accountability, cost-effectiveness, and integrity in the management and conduct of NIJ activities and programs.

Program Areas

In addressing these strategic challenges, the Institute is involved in the following program areas: crime control and prevention, including policing; drugs and crime; justice systems and offender behavior, including corrections; violence and victimization; communications and information technologies; critical incident response; investigative and forensic sciences, including DNA; less-than-lethal technologies; officer protection; education and training technologies; testing and standards; technology assistance to law enforcement and corrections agencies; field testing of promising programs; and international crime control.

In addition to sponsoring research and development and technology assistance, NIJ evaluates programs, policies, and technologies. NIJ communicates its research and evaluation findings through conferences and print and electronic media.

To find out more about the National Institute of Justice, please contact:

National Criminal Justice
 Reference Service
P.O. Box 6000
Rockville, MD 20849–6000
800–851–3420
e-mail: *askncjrs@ncjrs.org*